It's The Stories You Tell

That Color Your Life

Marylou Falstreau
&
Alan Falstreau
aka "The Crazy Ole Man"

Published and printed in the United States in 2009 by
Alan & Marylou Falstreau.

Second Edition - April 2009

Words by Alan Falstreau
Illustrated by Marylou Falstreau

For information write:

Marylou & Alan Falstreau
P O Box 13557
San Luis Obispo, Ca. 93406

or visit

www.TheCrazyOleMan.com
www.MFalstreau.com

ISBN: 1442110317 EAN-13 is 9781442110311.

To our sons Nathan and Matthew,

This book was written especially for you! It is our hearts desire to share the wisdom found in these beautiful messages. We believe they will help you on your journey through life, and with your permission we are sharing it with others.

You first knew us as Mom and Dad, but now we are Marylou and "The Crazy Ole Man!"

We love you!

And special thanks to our friend and editor on this project, Amanda de la Garza! Your insight, dedication and love have helped us make this project a wonderful reality.

Forward

It's the stories you tell yourself, along with the stories of those around you, that color your life. Remember to choose stories wisely and to paint with vibrancy and Joy!!

The power of your story
will lead you to freedom when
your story is created from deep
within... from a place that honors
your true nature.... that is
protected from the stories of
others... and is yours alone...
as it should be!

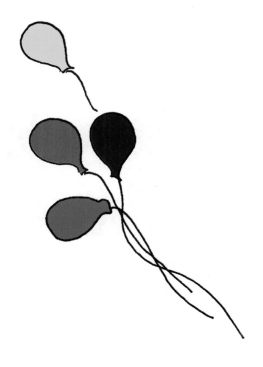

The day that you truly live what you believe, is the day that infinite miracles happen in the most surprising and magical ways.

Focus on the writing. Focus on living the story you desire. The signs are right... they are in place. Keep writing.

You define who you are by the stories you tell.

Tell stories of fun and joy that occur daily within the swirling chaos of the world around you. This has healing powers... both physically and spiritually.

Always share stories of fun and joy!!

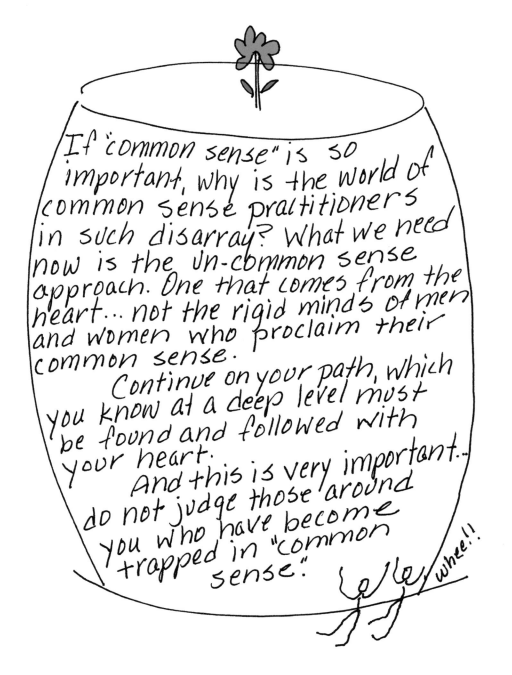

If "common sense" is so important, why is the world of common sense practitioners in such disarray? What we need now is the Un-common sense approach. One that comes from the heart... not the rigid minds of men and women who proclaim their common sense.

Continue on your path, which you know at a deep level must be found and followed with your heart.

And this is very important... do not judge those around you who have become trapped in "common sense."

whee!!

To see the beauty of a flower you must always acknowledge and _Thank_ the stem that supports it... the leaves that form it's body... and the unseen roots that stabilize it and provide it's path to nourishment.

So remember when you see a beautiful flower that there is much more to be thankful for than what first meets the eye. The same is true with each person you meet. See their unique beauty and know...

that there is much more... seen and unseen... to behold and understand.

It's not about who is right or wrong. Everybody is right or wrong in someone's story. So don't lose sleep over someone else's story if it doesn't match yours... for they are not necessarily wrong... nor are you.

The only thing that matters ultimately is... with the story you tell yourself, are you flowing peacefully along your journey? If the story you tell yourself is free of fear, worry, and criticism of others, you are.

This is how you know.

It is our limited
perspective that sees
limitation in ourselves
and others.

There is no security in the desire to have security... just the opposite. The focus on "having" betrays you. It's the feeling that there's never enough. Security in material things is fleeting. The only true security resides in your heart.

Anxiety and fear have nothing to do with the situations, people, places, or things you encounter.... but are sparked by the stories you tell about what appears in your life experience. For you see, these things, in and of themselves are neutral... neither good nor bad. It's your stories that label them as such.

You keep
the pain
alive by the
stories
you
tell.

See yourself on the mountaintop without those CNN labeled experts around you. What would your world look like? Much different, wouldn't it? The world is full of stories designed to make you feel bad...
don't listen.

The miracle of perfection within each moment oftentimes eludes you. Why you ask? Well wouldn't it, when your focus is always somewhere else... either in the future or the past—playing the part of victim or hero? Know this: there are no victims or heroes in the present moment. Only perfection.... and hopefully you.

The amazing thing about life is what you'll find if you just stop spinning and look. Be still and look. Be quiet and look. Just Be and look. There is so much to see and experience that is amazing from this perspective.

The stars become brighter... the sky becomes bluer... the birds sing much sweeter... the people in your life reveal gifts you had not noticed... when you are still... when you are quiet... when you are just present.

Experience... experience life if you desire joy and happiness. Wade into the water... you must wade into the water if you truly want to experience it. So it is with all of life.

Wade in.

There is no safety standing on the shore and dreaming what your life could be.

Never give up on the dream,
even if you can't totally decide what
it looks like... you know at a
deep level what it is. On a daily
basis just keep taking the steps.
This is how the dream becomes
defined.

The journey to the top of the mountain is not straight. It flows in many directions as you climb, with unknown vistas around each new turn. While your first reaction to a new view may be one of fear and worry... understand that it really is nothing more than just the next turn on the path and keep moving. Always, we emphasize, always keep moving.

Time is a manmade illusion. Don't fight it. What's your hurry, anyway??

Love
what you do,
and do what you
love... really well!
It's never about what
others may or may not
be doing. Focus on being
the very best you, with
an emphasis on
Being. The result
is being at
Peace.

Being Joyful.
Being in the
moment. Being
connected to the
infinite possibilities of
the infinite universe.

The nature of Nature is
to grow. You are part of Nature!
Grow where you are planted,
just as the flower seeds do...
find the nourishment you need
wherever you are.

A tree cannot grow into a bird... and a bird cannot grow into a tree. Both play a part in the growth of the other. But... very important to remember... the bird must understand its bird nature and a tree must appreciate its tree nature for growth to happen.

so it is for you.

Once, when you were small,
you thought of big things.
Now that you are big you
think of small things.
What's wrong with this picture?

Ask... always ask for what you desire from a position of love. When you do, you will be amazed by who hears and how magically they will respond.
For there are people... seen and unseen, and perhaps even long forgotten... who love you. And when you least expect it, they happily walk beside you.

Always ask from a position of love.

The magic that holds airplanes in the sky is within you. The magic that makes birds sing is within you. The magic that makes the dog's tail wag is within you. For you see... all these seemingly disconnected things...and you. are all one. One experience. Everything you experience is all related. It's just difficult for you sometimes to see the connection. As the dog's tail wags, the bird sings and the airplane flies...your life is impacted even when you don't understand now or why.

The biggest present you can give yourself is to send unconditional love to every creature. Unbelievable things will happen. And from where you least expect them will come the best surprises and most delightful gifts.

you
are never
alone, even
when your
eyes cannot see.
you are never
without support,
even when there
appears to be
none. You are
always loved,
even when you
perceive
pain and
chaos.

Celebrate today and the uniqueness you bring to the world. Help everyone also celebrate their uniqueness!

To provide for your needs and desires, come from a different perspective than most. Ask first.... how can I help .... how can I serve? For you see, this leads directly to the heart... and the heart leads directly to the abundance of the universe, where all that you need and desire is waiting for you! So don't get lost on the road as many do by thinking of themselves first. All journeys to abundance start by being there for someone else and asking, how may I help... how may I serve? Any other route leads to stress and frustration.

Oh, and by the way....
singing and dancing
along the way
really helps!

The same sun that rises
each day for you shines on all—
even those you do not see
or care to see. Their stories
are of equal value because we
are all connected... at different
levels and different times.
Never forget this.

Simplicity wins
every time. It is impossible
to complicate it. That is the
key to how it works! Even
those things that seem
complex are no more than
simple things linked
together in a pattern.
     Look for the pattern
because there lies the
simplicity you want.
     Life is not complicated...
it is only the stories you
tell about it that make it
so. It's the stories you
tell... see the pattern...
see how simple it
can be?

As you awake, see each day with a new set of eyes. Experience each day with a new touch of your hands. Feel the breeze on your face as if you are meeting a new friend for the first time. Hear birds as though they sing just for you. Yes, in this way you are truly alive in each moment.

When you open your eyes each morning, see beauty and light all around. When your feet first touch the ground, feel the energy flowing through you.

Look to nature for the answers to life's most pressing questions. Ask... how do they do that? The birds, the animals, the plants...getting up each new day and moving forward as if there were no yesterday...but only Today..

Watch the things of nature—they simply grow, facing the elements of the day...always to the best of their ability in each moment.

And so also with you... to the best of your ability in each moment... just grow...

Wiggle Your Toes!
When faced with a question or unknown situation, wiggle your toes! Then ask yourself, how did I do that?... What made my toes wiggle? Don't know the answer...that doesn't matter because you got your toes to wiggle, you achieved the desired result.
    Apply the same principle of not knowing the answer but gettings results to other questions or unknown situations. Wiggle your toes, and magically the results will appear. Because taking a moment to wiggle your toes moves you away momentarily and removes the blockage you faced, and allows you to move forward to solving the original question or solution.

when blocked... move..... and wiggle your toes!

Is it possible to walk through a door that is closed? The answer is yes, if you believe you can.

Think like others are unwilling to think, and the doors will open. It is only your story of fear that keeps you from doing so. Everyone has fear at some level... the secret is not to feed it.

Your dream is created much like writing a song, short story, or poem... from the heart. It is not formed by the influences of others or external circumstances. At times it is hard to define your dreams in words that others understand, but know that this makes the dream no less powerful or real.

Songs are sung in their time. Poems are read in their time. However, dreams can be accessed always... from the quiet places of your heart.

It's the love in your heart that makes the future bright.. not anything you can plan or design.

As you become aware, you can consciously raise your energy. As you raise your energy, you raise your spirit. As you raise your spirit, you raise the energy of those around you... whether they are aware of it or not. When they raise their energy your energy is raised even higher, along with the worlds. see the pattern?

Look for fun spots... they are everywhere, but they are not always obvious. Sometimes they hide hoping you will look for them... sort of a cosmic game of hide and seek.

They are not like rides at Disneyland... pre-programmed to entertain. You know you have found one when you smile for no reason. They are everywhere and they are always defined by you.

woo-
hoo!

Just Dance!!

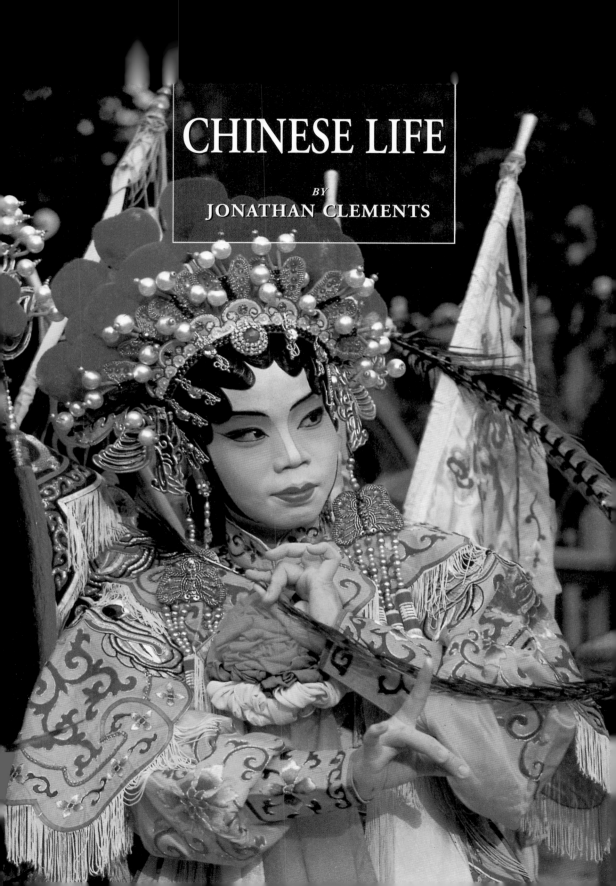

CHINESE LIFE

BY
JONATHAN CLEMENTS

Who Were the Ancient Chinese?

YANGSHAO CULTURE

The Yangshao people were one of the earliest recorded civilizations in China, thriving in around 4500 B.C. They lived in pyramid-shaped thatched huts, reared dogs and pigs, and made pottery. The tribes were ruled by women, property passed in the female line from daughter to daughter, and women had richer, better-furnished graves than their male counterparts.

China is big. It stretches from the frozen wastes of Siberia to the tropical islands of the Equator. Life was so precarious on the banks of its giant Yangzi and Yellow rivers, and the people so numerous, that whoever has wanted to rule part of China has been forced to seize, or try to seize, the whole. China's borders have changed constantly throughout the thousands of years of its civilization, which is one of the world's oldest and most advanced cultures. Originally made up of several squabbling states, the country was united in 221 B.C. when King Chen of Qin conquered his enemies and proclaimed himself the First Emperor. His family, or dynasty, ruled for only a few years until it was overthrown. Since then, each period of Chinese history has been named after the family that ruled it.

IMPERIAL RICHES

Since the Qin, there have been many different dynasties (ruling families), each claiming to rule the world on behalf of Heaven. The Chinese emperors' power was far reaching and brought them tribute taxes from all over Asia. Through the ages, their wealth attracted brilliant craftsmen, such as the creators of this Ming Dynasty vase.

THE LAST EMPEROR

Not all emperors were Chinese. The Yuan Dynasty members were Mongol invaders descended from Genghis Khan. The Manchurian Qing Dynasty ruled for more than 200 years. Its rule ended in 1912 when its Emperor Xuan Tong (personal name: Pu Yi) was ousted. Born in 1906 and made emperor at the age of 3, Pu Yi was to be the Last Emperor.

INNER & OUTER CHINA

China is commonly divided into two areas. Inner China, the area around the basins of the Yellow and the Yangzi rivers, is the core of the historical Chinese empire, and has sustained a continuous civilization since the Stone Age. Modern or Outer China includes Manchuria, Inner Mongolia, Xinjiang, and Tibet—vast areas of land that were considered by the Chinese to be foreign countries until relatively recently.

The historical Chinese empire
Modern China

THE MIDDLE KINGDOM

The Chinese name for their country is Zhong Guo (The Middle Kingdom), supposedly the center of the world. The symbol for middle consists of a line going straight through the center of a hole. The symbol for kingdom shows a king with a jewel, surrounded by a square to signify the borders of his kingdom.

EARLY MONEY

The bronze coin above (*c.* 220 B.C.) is circular to represent the Earth, with a square hole to represent Heaven. The symbol to the right of the hole means "shell," since earlier in the Shang Dynasty, cowrie shells were used as money. Early Chinese states soon developed their own currencies, including bricks of tea and metal chits. During the reign of the First Emperor, coins were standardized throughout the empire.

CHINESE DYNASTIES

2100–1600 B.C.
Xia Dynasty (Legendary)
1600–1100 B.C.
Shang Dynasty (North China only)
1100–221 B.C.
Zhou Dynasty (North China only)

IMPERIAL CHINA

221–207 B.C.
Qin Dynasty
206 B.C.–A.D. 220
Han Dynasty
220–280
Three Kingdoms Period
265–420
Jin Dynasty
420–589
Southern and Northern Dynasties (including Song, Qi, Liang, Chen, North, East & West Wei, North Qi, and Northern Zhou)
581–618
Sui Dynasty
618–907
Tang Dynasty
907–979
Five Dynasties and Ten Kingdoms
916–1125
Liao Dynasty
960–1279
Song Dynasty (North and South)
1115–1234
Kin Dynasty
1260–1368
Yuan Dynasty (Mongols take over)
1368–1644
Ming Dynasty
1644–1912
Qing Dynasty (Manchus take over)
1912
Last Emperor deposed

POST-IMPERIAL CHINA

1912–1949
Republic
1949–present day
People's Republic (Communist rule)

Life for the Rich

THE EXAM SYSTEM

In times of war, prowess on the battlefield could help someone rise through the ranks in society. In times of peace, the only way to advance was by becoming a civil servant. To do so, Chinese scholars had to take grueling exams consisting of memorized passages from poems and histories. But a passing mark only lasted for a limited period. They had to retake their exams regularly or they lost their qualifications.

Chinese society had a rigid hierarchy, with the emperor at the top and the common peasants at the bottom. Much of what remains of ancient China concerns the life of the rich and powerful, as only their artifacts have stood the test of time. Since the ancient Chinese invented paper, many of their documents have disintegrated faster than those of less advanced cultures whose documents were carved in stone or written on parchment. Few buildings remain standing, but artifacts found in graves have provided us with evidence of how people lived in ancient China.

CONSULTING THE ORACLE

Since the earliest days of the Shang dynasty (1600–1100 B.C.), those who could afford divine guidance sought it from a soothsayer. A hot pointer was pressed against the underpart of a tortoise shell while questions were asked. The cracks that formed were interpreted and the answers etched into the shell as a permanent record.

DECLINING NOBILITY

There were five ranks in ancient Chinese nobility, the Gong, Hou, Bo, Zi, and Nan, roughly equivalent to duke, marquis, earl, viscount, and baron. Chinese peerages were hereditary but declined over time. If a family did nothing to justify their honor, each successive generation would fall one rank, until the great-great-great grandson of the original nobleman became a humble commoner. However, the heir of Confucius (see page 28) always kept the highest rank.

A RICH MAN'S HOUSE

The layout of a person's house was said to directly affect the occupant's fortune. Those who could afford it would ensure that their house was positioned to avoid evil spirits and ill winds. The presence of other people's bad fortune could bring disaster, and the perfect gentleman's house was said to be in the quiet countryside; city dwelling was an evil to be avoided.

TOO RICH TO WORK

Long fingernails were a sign of a person who was wealthy enough not to have to do manual work. Many Chinese let at least one fingernail grow long but the very rich would grow all ten. Nail protectors were worn by the Qing Empress Dowager Zi Xi (1835–1908) to protect her long, carefully manicured nails.

THE SEAL OF AUTHORITY

Letters, documents, orders, and even paintings were marked with the owner's seal: a stylized representation of his or her name. Documents were not accepted as authentic without such a mark. Commoners and low-ranking officials would stamp in red, while high-ranking officials used mauve. During times of national mourning, all seals would use blue ink. Modern seals are roughly a centimeter square, but the emperor's official signature was so large it had to be lifted by two people.

MAGIC STONE

Jade was a prized commodity among the rich. Like all stone, it could be broken but never twisted, making it a symbol of honor and constancy. Jade was also rumored to have magical powers. An extremely difficult stone to shape, it had to be worn into the required form by laborious sanding.

Life for the Poor

Physical labor was a job for the poor and they were forced to become laborers, builders, and farmers to support the rich. Taxation was introduced in about 600 B.C., and peasants had to support wars by serving in the army or providing materials, food, and money. Peasant families relied heavily on those members who could work while dependents, such as old people and children, were a constant burden. But the old were looked after out of respect, and children were reared to share the work. Respect for elders lasted even after death when, in their afterlife, ancestors were believed to offer prayers to help and protect the family. Many peasants did not own their land. They were tenant-serfs of landlords who could punish them for not working hard enough, which meant they had little opportunity to earn extra money to buy land.

OX POWER

Ideally, an ox was used to pull a plow in the rice paddies. Oxen were not always easy to come by, as most animal herds were on the steppes of Outer China, whereas the farms were in Inner China. Some areas had "ox-lords" who rented out animals, but many peasants were too poor even to rent one, so they had to prepare their fields by hand.

LIFE IN THE CITY

It was considered bad feng shui (see pages 14–15) to live too close to others, as fates would become entwined.

The country was spacious, but less fortunate people had to live in crowded cities, sharing their neighbors' misfortunes. In both town and country, poor families lived together under one roof, often eating, sleeping, and living in the same room, and sometimes sharing it with their animals.

HARD LABOR

Chinese farm life was hard. In May and June each year there was a whirl of activity: planting, harvesting, moving young rice plants into the fields, and harvesting silk worms. Between November and February, with little to do, the large summer workforce became hungry mouths to feed. Working barefoot in rice paddies strewn with manure left the coolies (hired workers) prone to diseases. Such hardships led the Chinese to replace "coolie" with the words for bitterness and strength: kuli.

LAND LUBBERS

Those who were poor and who lived near the sea often became fishermen, a harsh job, with constant risk from pirate attack. Chinese fishermen rarely strayed far from the coast, and usually sailed in pairs for safety. A small Chinese boat is called a sampan, although today big and small boats both tend to be known as junks (from the Malay word, jong; large boat).

Food & Drink

China's vast size meant that its different regions were almost like foreign countries. Each had its own very different crops and dishes, and the distinctive styles of cooking still exist today. In south China, Cantonese food was cooked swiftly in hot oil; while farther north in the Yangzi Valley, more time was taken to prepare sweet-and-sour sauces. Unlike other regional cooking, Tibetan, Mongolian, and Manchurian cuisines used a lot of dairy products, whereas the coastal province of Fujian specialized in delicate seafood dishes. The distinctive spicy flavors of Sichuan cooking were only possible after the introduction of the Central American chili in the 16th century A.D.

CORMORANT FISHING

Rods and lines were not the only way to catch fish. Lamps on fishing boats lured fish to the surface where trained cormorants scooped them from the water. Each bird had a collar around its neck to prevent it from swallowing its catch. The fisherman forced the bird to spit the fish out, then sent it back into the water for more. Cormorant fishing is still practiced today.

RICE & RICE CULTURE

During the Tang dynasty (A.D. 618–907), quick-ripening varieties of rice were introduced from Vietnam. Canals built to aid transport and famine relief around China also brought water to outlying areas. It was lifted into the fields by a chain-and-paddle system operated by a turning crank. These changes, plus the development of new tools such as the harrow, made rice growing essential to feeding China's expanding population. But reliance on one food could cause trouble. If the rice crop failed, the famine affected the entire population.

WHEAT & MILLET

The staple food in ancient China was millet, which was ground into a kind of rough flour. Around A.D. 500, improvements in milling techniques made wheat more popular, and this formed the major ingredient in most noodle dishes.

ALL THE TEA IN CHINA

Tea, or *cha*, was a popular drink among both rich and poor, and was available in many different varieties to suit every taste and pocket. For the familiar red tea, the leaves were roasted. Other kinds, which used different flavorings and processes, could be sampled in a teahouse—a popular meeting place in ancient China. In the local dialect of south China, *cha* was pronounced *tay*, from which came the English word. All varieties of modern tea are descended from the Chinese original.

CHOPSTICKS

Metal was often in short supply, and so cooks in ancient China would cut up the food before it was brought to the table. The tiny bite-sized morsels were easy to pick up with wooden sticks, or chopsticks. The Chinese word for chopsticks is *kuaizi* (hasteners) because they hasten the food into the mouth. Chopsticks were used with a hand-held bowl so that the user could manipulate the food more easily.

A TASTE OF THE EXOTIC

Many exotic fruits and vegetables were grown in ancient China. They included lychee fruits (see left), longans (dragon's eyes), water chestnuts, snow peas, bitter melons, and Chinese cabbage (bak choi: "white vegetable"). All of these helped to give Chinese food its distinctive flavor and texture.

Pastimes

BOOK OF CHANGES

The I Ching is an ancient system of fortune-telling. Advice and answers to important personal questions were, and still are, sought by referring to a text, in which a chapter between 1 and 64 is consulted at random by throwing sticks or coins. The picture shows the eight three-line trigrams that are combined with one another to create the 64 numbers.

There were good and bad pastimes according to the Imperial government. Singing the praises of the emperor, watching approved dramas, and martial training were all thought to be good ways of strengthening the nation. Excessive drinking, gambling, and lewd behavior were all frowned upon. Plays that ridiculed the ruling dynasty were outlawed.

CHINESE CHESS

Chess was invented in India, but the Chinese had already adopted it by A.D. 570. Chinese chess is very different from the common version. It is played on a board of 64 squares, but the pieces move along the lines between them, and the kings cannot leave their four-square palaces. The 32 pieces are all the same size and shape, each one inscribed with its functions. As well as horses, chariots, ministers, and soldiers, the Chinese chessboard has elephants, guardsmen, and cannons.

CHINESE OPERA

Performances of music and song, popular since the 7th century A.D., eventually developed into Chinese opera. All the actors had to be male. They were divided into four classes of character, known as Sheng (emperors, generals, gentlemen), Qing (villains, rebels, outlaws), Dan (female roles), and Chou (comic relief).

READING THE FUTURE

Ancient China had its own unique systems for telling
fortunes, including face reading, which looked at
marks and lines on the face, and the I Ching.
Other systems developed over time, and palm
readers and astrologers could often be
found telling fortunes
on the streets.

BOOK OF SONGS

In order to report the mood of the people to the emperor, a
government agency called the Yue-fu was established in 120 B.C.
Its officials regularly traveled through the countryside writing
down the songs they heard. These reports survive as the Book
of Songs—perhaps the oldest pop charts in the world. Some of
the earliest Chinese instruments included stone chimes, bamboo
flutes, the *pipa* (lute), *huiqin* (fiddle),
and *qin* (zither), all of which
are illustrated here.

HIGH FLYING

As early as the 2nd century B.C., kites were
used for military signaling in China.
Physicians recommended kite flying as
an activity for young boys to make
them throw back their heads and
open their mouths, thereby cooling
the body's energy levels. Early kites
were shaped like a kite, the bird for
which they were named, but later
developments included dragon shapes
(that fought to cut each other's tails),
kites that could carry a human scout, and
exploding kites that carried firecrackers on
their strings. This modern kite looks like a
space-age version of a coiled dragon.

PUPPET MASTERS

Puppetry originated in China and is still a common form
of entertainment throughout Asia. But it was not just
entertainment. Puppetry once saved an emperor's life.
In 206 B.C., giant puppets were moved around on
the walls of a city in order to convince
the besieging rebels that Emperor
Gao Zi was still within. By the
time the ruse was discovered, he
had already made his getaway.

Fashion

Common people in ancient China mainly wore clothes made of hemp or ramie-grass. In the 14th century A.D., they began growing cotton brought in from South Asia, which was found to be warmer and more profitable to grow. Clothes were not just items to keep the body warm. They were important indicators of status, and high-ranking officials had to take great care with their appearance. Chinese clothes were often decorated with mythical animals to protect the wearer from harm and bring him or her good fortune. Most dragons were drawn with three or four claws on each limb. Five-clawed dragons were reserved for the Imperial family.

KEEPING COOL

Early fans were flat, rigid panels used by both men and women to keep cool. The folding variety was invented in Japan in the 4th century A.D., and eagerly adopted by the Chinese before the 11th century. It was important among the rich to have the right fan for the right season, and writing or painting on someone's fan was a sign of friendship. A deserted wife was called an "autumn fan."

THE SILK MYSTERY

Silk was one of China's most important commodities, and has been manufactured for well over 2,000 years. The silk road was the lengthy trade route between Asia and Europe, where Chinese silk was prized as early as Roman times. A light, soft fabric with a shimmering quality, silk was in great demand abroad, and foreign powers were desperate to know the secret of its manufacture. In the 6th century A.D., European spies managed to discover the incredible truth: it was made from a delicate gossamer thread unwound from the cocoons of silkworm moths.

MEN OF THE CLOTH

Mandarins and other officials had to wear elaborate clothing and jewels to show their rank. But monks and priests took a vow of poverty and wore very simple, humble robes.

MANDARIN STYLE

From the 12th century onward, the Manchu people of northern China began to create fashions to honor their most faithful servant, the horse. These styles eventually caught on in other parts of China. Sleeves were worn wide and placed over the hands to resemble the horse's hoof, and servants were made to wear their hair shaven at the front and plaited in the back, to resemble a horse's tail.

HIGH & MIGHTY

A mandarin was a member of any of the senior grades of bureaucracy. His footwear kept him high above lesser mortals, and away from troublesome dirt. Such shoes could be difficult to walk in, but only a peasant or common laborer would need to get himself about. The richer the mandarin, the more likely he was to be carried everywhere!

FOOT BINDING

Small feet were considered a sign of beauty – the smaller the better. From around A.D. 1000, girls had their feet tightly bound to help increase their chances of getting a good husband. Eventually the instep broke, creating a kind of gnarled hoof. Walking was agony, yet poets praised the deformed results of foot binding as "golden lilies." This tradition continued in China until the early 20th century.

Art & Architecture

FINE FIGURES

FINE FIGURES

Sculpture was highly regarded from early times. This white earthenware horse was found in the grave of Zhang Shigui, a nobleman from the Tang Dynasty (A.D. 618–907).

The wealth and sophistication of ancient China created some of the most valuable treasures in the world. In times when the empire was strong and stable, such as at the height of the Sung and Tang dynasties, Chinese arts flourished in every conceivable medium, including bronze statuary, silken textiles, lacquer work, ink paintings, and decorated porcelain. Chinese architecture avoided hard edges and corners in favor of soft curves as seen in the winglike shape of Chinese roofs. It was believed that this softer style created good qi (energy). A similar emphasis on flowing shapes and natural harmony is found in the other arts. Chinese painters often concentrated on landscape scenes of shan shui (mountains and water), with swirling mists and tiny human figures dwarfed by the beauty of nature.

FENG SHUI

Feng shui (wind and water) is that which can be felt but not seen, grasped but not held. Originally used to find auspicious sites for graves in the 3rd century A.D., this set of beliefs and superstitions was adapted to help the living counter unlucky influences in their homes. Even today, feng shui masters use a complex compass, such as this one, to determine the lucky and unlucky influences caused by the position of a house.

BRONZE AGE ART

The Shang people flourished in north China around 1000 B.C., and were incredibly advanced forgers of bronzeware which they decorated with images of mythical monster masks and animal figures. Some pictures were broken up into square thunder-pattern spirals, or leiwen, with just an eye remaining to indicate it symbolized a living creature.

THE FORBIDDEN CITY

The capital city of China, Beijing, was designed along regular, square, grid patterns, which were good for transport. The north-south and east-west alignment of the square deliberately evoked the feng shui of ancient times. In 1420 a walled citadel was built in the middle as a home for the emperor and his family. Closed to outsiders, it was known as the Forbidden City.

Health & Medicine

Chinese medicine is based on herbal cures and the theory of qi—an energy believed to be in all living things. A person's qi had to be kept healthy and balanced, otherwise he or she would fall ill. Qi was kept good through eating a healthy diet and getting sufficient exercise. However, while the ancient Chinese had medical beliefs, they lacked medical science. Some cures worked by accident, while others did more harm than good. No system was in place to prove those cures that worked and those that didn't. Matters were not helped by shyness; doctors could not touch female patients, and instead had to use a doll to indicate where the pain was.

MOXIBUSTION

Some aches and pains were treated with moxibustion, which involved making pastilles from the dried leaves of the moxa plant, applying them to the skin and setting them on fire (normally under a glass to contain the heat). This practice is still in use today.

MAN ROOT

Ginseng, which became widespread after the 12th century A.D., is an aromatic root, often shaped like a man and highly prized for its medicinal properties. All ginseng in China was considered the property of the emperor, though he would often bestow quantities of it upon his loyal subjects. It was believed that the ginseng plant would turn into a white-blooded man if left undisturbed for 300 years and that the blood of such a man could raise the dead.

ACUPUNCTURE

The Chinese believed that energy circulated throughout the body but could be unbalanced if the channels became locked. In about A.D. 1, the science of acupuncture was devised to treat this problem. It involved sticking needles into the body at special points as shown on this statue. Still in use today, it is thought to stimulate the body's own defense systems, and is also used as an anesthetic.

OPIUM WARS

Opium was widely used in China as a painkiller, but was put to other uses during the late Ming Dynasty (1368–1644). With the arrival of tobacco from America, people began to smoke a mixture of the two drugs. Listless, weak opium addicts became a major problem, and the drug was banned. However, large quantities arrived with British traders, who used it to pay for tea. In 1840, this led to the Opium War, which ended with China's defeat and Britain's occupying Hong Kong as part of the settlement.

MORNING EXERCISE

The Chinese have always believed that exercise and clean living strengthen the body's energy and extend the natural lifespan. One such exercise was tai qi, a combined regime of calisthenics that could also be used as a martial art. Strengthening the body, it was said, would also strengthen the mind. Other physical exercises included gong-fu boxing, which we know today as kung fu.

MYSTERY CURES

The lack of scientific method in Chinese medicine has meant that some cures work well, whereas others are merely based on superstition. Deer horns were imported in vast quantities for use in medicines, most probably because the word in Chinese for deer sounds a little like "ease" in some dialects.

Love & Marriage

LOVE BIRDS

Because Mandarin ducks mate for life they have become the Chinese symbol of a loving and faithful marriage. Wild geese in flight were the symbols of communication from afar. They crop up in many poems about lovers forced to live apart, waiting for news of each other.

In ancient China people were expected to put their family duty ahead of their personal feelings. Marriages were arranged by professional matchmakers, sometimes before the bride and groom were even born. Such alliances turned enemies into in-laws who were then obliged to respect and help each other. A bride had to leave her family behind and become a member of her husband's family. In her new home, she would have to worship his ancestors and obey his parents.

SECOND-CLASS WIVES

A man could have only one wife who would share any title or honors he gained during his life. However, he was free to take concubines to increase his chances of having more children. As a second-rank "wife," a concubine was liable to be badly treated by both her husband's mother and his first wife.

DIVORCE

A man could divorce his wife if she were barren, stole anything, neglected to honor her in-laws, or even if she talked too much. However, he could not divorce her during mourning, if he had come into money, or if she had no home to return to. This weathered, ancient Chinese illustration depicts a couple arguing.

FATAL ATTRACTION

The most beautiful woman in Chinese history was said to be Yang Guifei, an 8th century companion of the Emperor Xuanzong. He was so infatuated with her that he neglected his kingdom and appointed members of her family to high offices. The last straw came when he made her cousin prime minister. There was a rebellion and she was killed.

MARRIAGE RITUALS

Before a marriage took place, the year, month, day, and hour of the bride and groom's birth were checked to ensure that the union would bring good fortune. On the chosen (lucky) day, the bride wore red and was taken to the groom's home in a sedan chair. The pair worshipped the groom's ancestors together, leaving the shrine as man and wife. Until the beginning of the Sui Dynasty (A.D. 605), Chinese women had to wear veils when they went outside the house. This custom is still practiced at many Chinese weddings today.

LU'S LOVE LOST

The Zhinan temple complex in Taiwan is sacred to Lu Dongbin, one of the eight Immortals of Chinese legend, who was thwarted in love. It is unlucky for lovers to visit the temple together, lest they be parted by the Immortal's jealous anger.

Women & Children

According to ancient Chinese philosophy the universe was a place in constant search of harmony and balance. As applied to men and women it was considered the man's duty to command and the woman's duty to obey. Real life, however, wasn't so simple. Women could exert great authority over their children, and several emperors were puppets of their powerful mothers. Though sworn to obey her husband, a wife was the boss at home. Even the philosopher Confucius once complained: *"When she's close, she's insolent. When she's far away, she nags."*

POMEGRANATE

A pomegranate is a fruit bursting with seeds, and so became a Chinese symbol of fertility. Pomegranates were placed in the homes of couples who hoped to have more children. However, couples who already had too many mouths to feed tried to avoid them at all costs.

THE EMPRESS DOWAGER

The Empress Dowager Zi Xi (1835–1908) was the last of many female rulers, stretching back to the 1st century A.D., who put a weakling on the throne so she could rule from behind the scenes. The weakling in question was her own son, the Tongzhi Emperor. Although an emperor was all-powerful, he was still obliged to obey his surviving parents, and sometimes a mother could use her power over her son to rule the whole nation.

UNICORN FATE

The Chinese unicorn, or jilin, was said to have appeared shortly before the death of Confucius, and to herald a time of great peace and prosperity. A unicorn is thought to bring luck to parents in the form of a genius child, and images of them were often kept near cradles. Such legends of fantastical creatures were reinforced when Admiral Zheng-He brought back a giraffe from his sea journey to Africa, and astounded the Chinese court.

CELESTIAL BIRDS

As the dragon was the symbol of the male, the phoenix was the symbol of the female. Phoenix designs can be found on many articles of female clothing and jewelry throughout Chinese history.

CHILDREN

Children were expected to work from a very young age. Peasant sons worked in the fields with their parents. Children as young as seven were given adult tasks and responsibilities. Chinese ages were counted from one, not zero, so children were one year old the moment they were born. Instead of having birthdays, everyone would add a year to their age at each Chinese New Year, so it was technically possible for a child born on New Year's Eve to be two years old the following morning.

SILK SPINNING

While their brothers were in the fields, girls had to spin and weave. A poor family dreaded the birth of a girl. She would be one more mouth to feed until they could marry her off, at which point they would have to pay a dowry to her prospective husband's family. Whatever happened, the bride rarely had much say in her fate. According to Confucian tradition, a girl was supposed to obey her parents until she married, her husband until his death, and her eldest son until her own death.

ALIEN INVADERS

The Great Wall didn't always work. In the 4th century A.D., it was crossed by the Tabgatch people of Inner Mongolia, who founded the Wei Dynasty. In the 12th century, the people of the steppes were united under their strongest ruler ever, Genghis Khan. His grandson Kublai conquered China and founded the Yuan Dynasty in 1271. It was breached for the last time in the 17th century, when the Manchus invaded and stayed to rule China right up until the early 20th century.

ARMOR

Robes restricted movement, so Chinese soldiers wore trousers to make horseback riding easier. Tough leather protected most parts of the body, with extra quilting to reduce the impact of blows. Cavalrymen wore extra leg protection. Metal plates were uncommon, except on the chest in later years. Most soldiers wore small metal studs to deflect enemy blades. Chinese soldiers often painted a tiger's head on their shields, or even wore imitation tiger skins, complete with a fake tail. As "King of Beasts," an image of the tiger was meant to strike fear into the hearts of China's enemies.

CLAY SOLDIERS

We know a great deal about Chinese warfare from the evidence found at archaeological sites, especially the Qin Emperor's famous Terracotta Army. It consisted of over 6,000 lifelike statues guarding his tomb. Most of the soldiers, however, are empty-handed. The real weapons they had carried were looted during a rebellion in 206 B.C.

War & Weaponry

In some parts of China the climate will support only farming; in others, only herding. The northern border zone supports both, and so throughout history, it has been fought over constantly. The greatest threats to China came from the plains of Asia, from horseback-riding tribes such as the Mongols and the Xiong-nu (Huns). China's soldiers had advanced weaponry to fight off the barbarian (foreign) invaders. Iron weapons replaced inferior bronze during the 7th century B.C., around the time that the Chinese invented the crossbow. From 500 B.C., horses were ridden instead of simply being used to pull chariots. Triple ranks of archers and crossbowmen kept up a continuous rain of arrows; charioteers and horsemen charged through enemy ranks; and humble footsoldiers attacked with swords and spears.

FIRE POWDER

Gunpowder was first used in fireworks during the 7th century A.D. Today, firecrackers are still used to scare off evil spirits at important occasions. Some were also used for military purposes, fired into enemy ranks to cause chaos. Actual guns of Western origin were first used in China by Mongol invaders under Genghis and Kublai Khan.

GREAT WALL

The First Emperor ordered the Great Wall of China to be built as a defense against invasion by the nomadic tribes of the plains beyond China. Overall, it was about 4,000 miles (6,000 km) long and had a series of watchtowers along its length. Although parts of it date from the 3rd century B.C., the most famous views we see are those restored in the Ming Dynasty during the 15th and 16th centuries. At its western end, it is little more than a bank of mud.

POMP & CEREMONY

Not all weapons were for warfare. This Shang-Dynasty axe has a bronze handle and a blade of jade which would not have been much use in battle. More likely, it was used for ceremonial purposes. A jade blade was believed to have magical properties.

Crime & Punishment

Chinese judges would have had images of cranes in their courtrooms, and the bird eventually became a symbol of justice itself.

Several types of punishment were used against wrongdoers in ancient China. The mildest were flogging or being locked into wooden stocks. The next level involved banishment, either for a limited period or permanently. A death sentence also varied with the severity of the crime. The simplest method was a straightforward beheading, but truly evil criminals (such as those who had murdered their parents) were treated to the terrible "lingering death," by which they were slowly cut to pieces while still alive.

STREET WISE

Strict rules governed the right-of-way on Chinese streets. Pedestrians had to make way for coolies carrying heavy loads. Coolies had to make way for empty sedan chairs. Empty sedan chairs had to make way for occupied sedans. Chairs had to make way for horses, and *everyone* had to make way for a wedding procession or an important official. Because it was polite to dismount to greet friends, pedestrians often used a fan to hide their face from acquaintances who were on horseback or in a sedan chair. Otherwise, the friend would be obliged to get down to say hello.

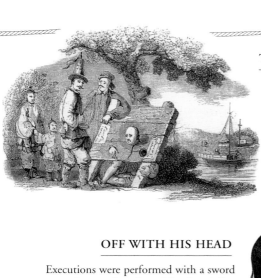

THE CRIMINAL'S YOKE

Petty thieves and other minor criminals were forced to wear a heavy wooden collar called a cangue. It was generally taken off at night, but during the day they would have to rely on their friends for help, as they couldn't feed themselves.

OFF WITH HIS HEAD

Executions were performed with a sword that was heavily weighted to deliver the cleanest and swiftest downward stroke possible. An executioner's sword was too unwieldy for use in combat; it was only good for chopping off heads.

CANING

Some criminals were flogged with a lash made from a strip of bamboo that had been planed smooth. There were two kinds of instruments, the heavy and the light, and the criminal would be struck across the back. However, Emperor Kang Xi of the Qing Dynasty decreed that beating the buttocks was preferable, as there was less risk of damaging internal organs.

METHODS OF TORTURE

Magistrates were allowed to use torture to extract confessions. Men were flogged, and women could be slapped on the cheeks with a piece of leather. Chinese water torture involved the slow dripping of water onto the victim, who was usually wrapped in a cloth. As it slowly became soaked it made it almost impossible for the person to breathe. There was also a device for squeezing the fingers or the ankles until the bones rubbed together painfully.

WHEELBARROWS

The earliest plans for the Chinese wheelbarrow date back to the 1st century A.D. With the wheel under the main part, it could easily lift 300 pounds (135 kg) of weight, and was used extensively to replace a cart on narrow tracks.

WATER CLOCKS

Time was kept with a clepsydra or water clock, which originally consisted of several jars. They each emptied after a set time, and more exact measurements could be made with a bamboo dipstick to see how much water (and time) was remaining. Water clocks are a very old invention in China, but were not mentioned in literature earlier than the 1st century B.C.

PAPER, PULP, & PARCHMENT

Though a form of parchment was in use in China during the Han Dynasty, the legendary inventor of paper was Cai Lun, who died in A.D. 114. He is said to have made his first sheets from old linen, tow, and pieces of fishnet. Paper made from rice straw or bamboo pulp was used in the normal way. Stronger papyrus sheets were used in windows as a cheap alternative to glass. It was considered extremely bad luck to step on paper inscribed with words, or even to throw it away. It had to be carefully burned to avoid ill fortune. The picture shows the fresh wet paper being laid out on racks to dry in the sun.

THE BURNING OF THE BOOKS

In 213 B.C., the Qin Emperor, on advice from his prime minister, decided to burn all records of previous dynasties and all books that were not for soothsaying or of medical or agricultural use. The Qin Dynasty was believed to be so great that no previous literature could be of interest. Important and irreplaceable documents and records of discoveries were burned. This also helped the Qin Emperor control what the population read. Hundreds of people were burned alive when they were found to be hiding books. Books from before this period have only survived by accident. Several hundred years later, in the Liang Dynasty, Emperor Yuan burned another 140,000 books for similar reasons.

Transport & Science

Despite occasional disasters, such as the Burning of the Books, the Chinese were an advanced civilization. In warfare they had crossbows and fireworks, and in industry they were using water wheels to power bellows in forges as early as the 1st century A.D. But "science," as a method of improving earlier ideas, was almost unknown. In later centuries, China was limited by its own education system. Even in the 19th century, the only way to get ahead was by studying the classics, and officials frowned upon people with knowledge of new-fangled arts like engineering, steam trains, or medicine.

COUNTING BOARDS

Mathematics in China was done with an abacus, or counting board, often said to be a primitive form of computer. Each row represents units, tens, hundreds, thousands and so on, and calculation can be as fast as with a pen and paper. But, with pen and paper it's possible to check back for mistakes. Our word abacus comes from the Hebrew for dust (abak) on a tabletop, in which people wrote their sums.

CATCHING QUAKES

The scientist Zhang Heng invented this earthquake detector in A.D. 132. An internal pendulum would knock against the sides if there was a tremor, causing a ball to fall from a dragon's mouth into a frog's mouth. Exactly which frog caught which ball would show the direction of the quake. A year before his death in A.D. 138, Zhang used the device to detect an earthquake 373 miles away.

SEDAN CHAIRS

Important officials would be carried in a sedan chair by a team of men. The emperor was allowed sixteen bearers, princes and governors had eight, and other officials had four. Others who could afford it were only permitted two.

DAOISM

Daoism was founded in the 6th century B.C. by Lao Zi. It was a philosophy that preached harmony in all things, represented by the uniting of chaos and law, negative and positive, and earth and sky in the yin-yang symbol.

Religion

*I*n ancient China, it was considered rude to impose upon those who were too high above or far below oneself in rank, and this even applied in the afterlife. Worshippers could only pray to their ancestors and family, or spirits of a similar class. The Chinese believed that the next world was very like our own, and that they could send aid to their ancestors by burning paper effigies in the real world.

The emperor prayed to the most powerful gods, to keep the land free of flood and famine. Natural disasters were sometimes used as excuses for revolts, blamed on an emperor who was failing in his divine duties. As in China today, there was no single religion, but several belief systems which existed side-by-side.

CONFUCIANISM

Confucius sought to make the world a better place with precise rules on a small scale. He thought that if each person knew their place in the family, then each village, city, and province would be strengthened, and ultimately the entire state would become perfect. Confucianism preached loyalty and respect to one's ancestors.

BUDDHISM

Buddhism first arrived in China, from India, in the 1st century A.D., though there are earlier stories about Buddhist missionaries imprisoned by the Qin Emperor and rescued by an angel. Initially an urban religion, it slowly spread into the countryside as believers mixed it with elements of Daoism. Buddhists believe that you can only be truly happy when you stop wanting things and work to remove all desire from your life. Their ultimate aim is to achieve enlightenment through reincarnation.

BURNING INCENSE

Incense is made from the dust of certain sweet-smelling woods, mixed with clay. The sticks then burn slowly to fill the air with their perfume; some were even marked to show the passing of time. In ancient China, incense was burned as a way of honoring the gods.

HOROSCOPES

Chinese horoscopes were an important part of everyday life. Fortune-tellers would ascertain which of twelve different animals ruled the year of someone's birth. The animals were the Rat, Ox, Tiger, Rabbit, Dragon, Snake, Horse, Sheep, Monkey, Rooster, Dog, and Pig, after which time the cycle would return to the Rat. The year 2000 was ruled by the Dragon, so you can count forward or backward to work out which animal rules you.

FOREIGN FAITHS

Buddhism is not the only foreign import. Many of China's ethnic groups have their own beliefs, including thousand-year-old communities of Christians and Muslims. This is the Potala palace, the former home of the religious leader of Tibet, the Dalai Lama.

EVIL SPIRITS

The magical art of feng shui sought to protect the living from predatory ghosts and evil spirits. It was believed that symbolic guardians could keep supernatural threats at bay, hence statues like this fearsome stone lion, found outside a Chinese tomb.

Legacy of the Past

GOOD MEDICINE

The positive aspects of Chinese medicine, such as herbalism and acupuncture, have spread throughout the world. Today, it is rare for a city to be without at least one shop selling traditional Chinese remedies.

The greatest legacy of ancient China is modern China. Unlike many other past civilizations, it is still with us today, bigger and more powerful than before. But there are many different Chinas. There is the ancient historical civilization, the vast Communist state, the "little dragon" Chinese nations like Singapore and Taiwan, and the millions of people all around the world who are ethnic Chinese. There are no emperors any more, but China is still a great superpower and central in world politics and trade. The people still call their nation Zhong Guo, "the Middle Kingdom."

HONG KONG

Taken by the British after the Opium War, Hong Kong was returned to China in 1997. In the interim, it had grown into a center of commerce, the tiny area of land turning into a forest of skyscrapers. This giant building is owned by the Bank of China, and was designed in accordance with the rules of feng shui. Some locals disagreed, suggesting that it looked like a giant dagger: very bad luck.

THE BALLAD OF MULAN

In the 6th century A.D., songs were sung about Hua Mulan ("Magnolia Flower"), a girl who joined the army in her father's place. She fought for 12 years disguised as a man, but when she was offered a place in the Khan's court (China at the time was ruled by foreign Tabgatch nomads), she begged instead to be given a camel on which she could ride home to her family. The story is still famous today.

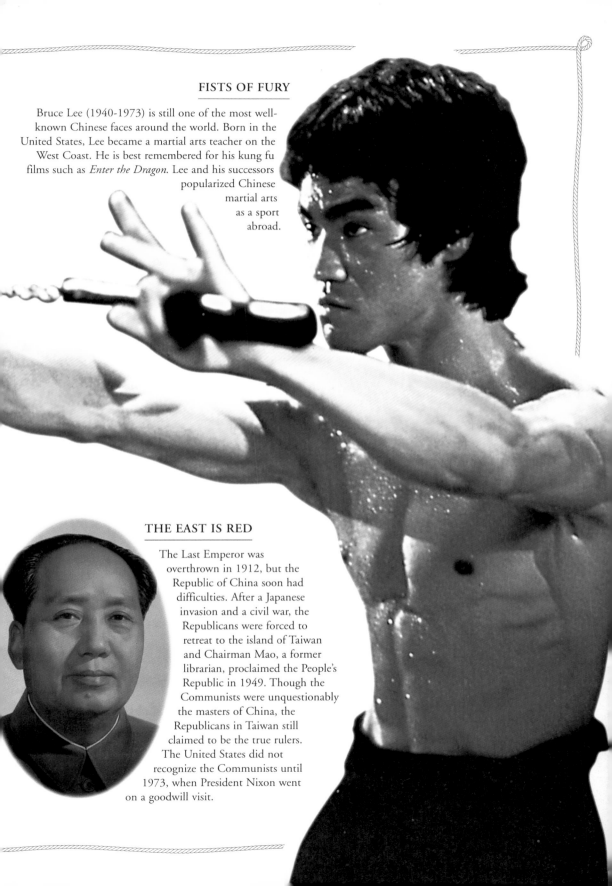

FISTS OF FURY

Bruce Lee (1940-1973) is still one of the most well-known Chinese faces around the world. Born in the United States, Lee became a martial arts teacher on the West Coast. He is best remembered for his kung fu films such as *Enter the Dragon*. Lee and his successors popularized Chinese martial arts as a sport abroad.

THE EAST IS RED

The Last Emperor was overthrown in 1912, but the Republic of China soon had difficulties. After a Japanese invasion and a civil war, the Republicans were forced to retreat to the island of Taiwan and Chairman Mao, a former librarian, proclaimed the People's Republic in 1949. Though the Communists were unquestionably the masters of China, the Republicans in Taiwan still claimed to be the true rulers. The United States did not recognize the Communists until 1973, when President Nixon went on a goodwill visit.

DID YOU KNOW?

There are thousands of Chinese characters?
The total number of Chinese characters and variants is estimated at 40,000, though nobody could possibly list or learn them all. The majority are ancient, extinct words or extremely complex ideas in specialist fields. To reach a reasonable level of Chinese reading ability, you would need to memorize a much smaller number: maybe just 5,000.

That martial artists once fought a war against Christians? Christianity took root in parts of China from A.D. 631. When organized bands of missionaries arrived many centuries later, the locals were heard to complain that the sharp church spires erected by the "Jesus devils" upset the area's feng shui. Toward the close of the Qing dynasty in 1899, poor areas saw the Boxer Rebellion against Christianity and all other foreign influences. The Boxers were martial artists who claimed to have a magic invulnerability to foreign blades and bullets. Some would enter trances to be possessed by the God of War.

That goldfish are baby dragons? According to some Chinese tales, a goldfish turns into a dragon when it dies and passes through the Gates of Heaven. It will return to wreak vengeance if owners have mistreated it, or grant them great fortunes if they were kind to it.

Gold and silk can kill? In ancient Chinese records, if people were said to have "swallowed gold" it meant they drank poison and killed themselves. If an official was "presented with silk," it was a command from the Emperor that he should be strangled.

Midnight guessing games were banned? Chai Mui is a game played by two people holding up a hand each, with some, all, or none of the fingers displayed, and simultaneously shouting out a guess at the sum of the two hands. The closest guess is the winner. During the Qing Dynasty, games of Chai Mui became so loud that the Governor of Hong Kong banned them between 11 P.M. and 6 A.M.

PRONUNCIATION

Most of the Chinese words in this book sound as they look to you.
The following letters are pronounced differently:

c = ts, I = ee after all consonants except c, ch, s, z, and zh, when it sounds like yrrh.

q = ch, x = hs (pronounced fast), **z = dz, zh = j**

First edition for the United States, its territories and dependencies, Canada, and the Philippine Republic, published 2000 by Barron's Educational Series, Inc.
Original edition copyright © 2000 by Ticktock Publishing, Ltd.
U.S. edition copyright © 2000 by Barron's Educational Series, Inc.

All inquiries should be addressed to: Barron's Educational Series, Inc., 250 Wireless Boulevard, Hauppauge, New York 11788, **http://www.barronseduc.com**
Library of Congress Catalog Card No. 99-68836   International Standard Book No. 0-7641-1070-5
Picture research by Image Select.
Printed in Spain   9 8 7 6 5 4 3 2 1

Picture Credits:
t=top, b=bottom, c=center, l=left, r=right, OFC=outside front cover, IFC=inside front cover, IBC=inside back cover, OBC=outside back cover

AKG Photos: 4bl, 4tl, 5tl, 9t,9br, 11tr, 11cl, 13br, 16bl, 17t, 24cr, 25tr, 26tr & OBC bc, 26/27c, 27bl, 28/29c, OFC (main pic) & OFCcr. Ancient Art & Architecture Collection: 2tl, 2bl, 3br, 4cb, 12bl, 21tr, 21bl, 25tl, 27tr, 29cl, 29tr. The British Museum: 18br. Ann Ronan @ Image Select: 2/3c, 6tr, 6/7, 13tr & OBC cr, 14/15, 20cr, 20/21cr, 28bl, 32c. Corbis: 4c, 10cl, 12tl, 13cl, 17br, 20tl, 25br. e.t. archive: 8cr, 19tr, 22tl, OFCtr, OFCtc & OFCbr. Heather Angel: 16tl. Holt Studios International: 8bl, 9bl. The Hutchinson Library: 18/19c. Images Colour Library: 10tl, 14/15tr, 16/17c. Image Select: 6bl, 6br, 22bl, 23bl, 26bl, 29tl, 30br, 31bl. Jean Loup Charmet: 26c. Oxford Scientific Films: 18tl, 24tl. Ronald Grant Archive: 30bl, 31. Science & Society: 27br. Spectrum: 10/11c & IFC, 11cr, 17cl, 19br, 23tr. Still Pictures: 30tr. Tony Stone Images: 8tl & OBCtr, 22cr. Werner Foreman Archive: 5tr, 11br, 12/13c, 20bl, 23b, 29br. 24/25c *Everyday Life through the Ages* by Reader's Digest.

Every effort has been made to trace the copyright holders and we apologize in advance for any unintentional omissions.
We would be pleased to insert the appropriate acknowledgment in any subsequent edition of this publication.

BARRON'S